I0152749

In the Garden of Angels and Demons

In the Garden of Angels and Demons

Poems by

Stephen Anderson

Kelsay Books

© 2017 Stephen Anderson. All rights reserved. This material may not be reproduced in any form, published, reprinted, recorded, performed, broadcast, rewritten or redistributed without the explicit permission of Stephen Anderson. All such actions are strictly prohibited by law.

ISBN 13- 978-1-945752-63-6

Kelsay Books
Aldrich Press
www.kelsaybooks.com

Acknowledgments

Grateful acknowledgment goes to the following publications in which these poems first appeared.

New Purlieu Review: "A Tribute to the Penguin-Men Among Us"

The Silent Tango of Dreams (Pudding House Publications, 2006): "The House Alongside," "Woodland Sojourn," "A Gift of Lavender," "On the Glades Near Strawberry Fields," "Desert Walk," "The Privileged Secrets of the Arch," "The Myth of Red in Amsterdam," "On a Hot Afternoon in Jerusalem," "Third Planet," "The Rebel Nymph," "The Special Hunter"

Wisconsin Poets' 2002 Calendar: "Basilica circa 2000 A.D."

Tipton Poetry Journal: "Basilica circa 2000 A.D."

Verse Wisconsin: "Reminiscence on a Sunday Afternoon" "Flight 006"

Portals and Piers (Sunday Morning Press, 2012): "On Meeting Again" "Westward"

Foundling Review: "The Laying of Hands"

Fox Cry Review: "Legacy", "At the Oriental Theater in Milwaukee"

Southwest Review: "Copper Dream"

Brawler: "Nighthawk," "The Meaning of It"

Harvests of New Millennium: "Blocked"

Free Verse: "Falling to Heaven", "Epitaph on A Late-Winter Mouse," "Detour," "A View from Above"

Your Daily Poem: "A Discovery"

Tipton Poetry Journal: "The Signal"

The Milwaukee Journal Sentinel: "The List"

Art Night Books: "Rome, July 2012"

Navigating in the Sun (Finishing Line Press, 2015): "Desert Walk," "Horizon," "Hurricane," "Reverie," "Things Said" "A First Time for Everything," "In Style"

The Journey (2015): Art book by Christine E. Alfery in which "Of the First Magnitude" was selected to appearwith one of the paintings in the book.

Contents

III.

About the Author

There are no facts, only interpretations.
—Friedrich Wilhelm Nietzsche

I.

A Discovery

Last spring, the old bay window over the back deck was
Done in by ripsaw, crowbar and sledgehammer—
Smashed into a pile of scattered debris on the deck.
Among the leftovers, in the middle of a boxed-in section,
A hornets' nest rose up, a Taj Mahal dome in miniature, some ten
Inches in diameter, a delicate looking carp scale pattern of maple
Seed and other unknown matter, home, the carpenter said,
To scores of yellow jackets many of which terrorized us in
Seasons past while we entertained on the deck.

When the nest was torn open, its interior was empty like
Some lost, ancient civilization once sheltered so well by its
Intricate design. Now gone forever from our property, a sacrifice
To our sliding deck door, a weatherproof invention—
Man-made technology of high order, lacking, though, the
Miracle that preceded it in that spot.

The Privileged Secrets of the Arch

Of all of those in the park, only
The rosy-cheeked, disheveled woman saw the
Poltergeists weave under and
Around the monumental park arch, so much
So that she dropped her plastic bag
Filled with everything she owned
And cherished, thereby setting her
Hands free to applaud them as they
Set about in their anarchistic abandon
Magically whirling debris with whistling sounds,
Creating traces of colored lines that were
Utterly magnificent for this lone observer
To behold. What a shame – she thought –
That she must relish in this free performance
Art alone. And how blessed she considered herself
That only she could enjoy such a gift in her
Own dusty, litter-strewn amusement park while
Others there could content themselves with just
Simply staring at her.

Nighthawk

It's 3 AM outside the 7-Eleven.
In the distance, approaching car headlights
Dot the blackness at this hour while
Inside a scrawny twenty-something sits
Behind the counter tracing a 9 mm under the
Counter with his fingers, surrounded by four lonely
Walls that contain items insomniacs seek
During black hours like these. All the cars
Pass silently except for one that booms by, its radio
blasting—
A rolling boom box that shatters the still,
Vapid night air while the car's occupants
Head to nowhere good, to their rendezvous
With the nothingness of this night rhythm
In the key of absurd loneliness.
They all seem to head toward what home
Might be, the place where eyes will later
Strain under desk lamp far into the night
Amid silver ghosts that shimmer in the dark blue
Shadows before sleep envelops them in a dream
Of star-sent angels light years from Edward Hopper's
Nighthawks, while outside the night's mist will soon start
To evaporate, as it will again and again . . . .

A First Time for Everything

Did you really notice
the pattern,
the colors,
the images or,
the stories?

Did you
look at,
study,
listen to

the song the object makes?

If not,
it's there—a
communication with colors,
both broad and fine stroked,
pitched and kilned
into
the jewel that sings

in its fine glaze there—right
in front of you.

There can be a first time for everything.

Third Planet

Ocher hills with withered parched
Trees, dry-as-bone stream beds,
Mysteriously placed Stonehenge-like monoliths,
Rusted steel sheets,
Concrete and metal constructions,
Lunatic war contraptions and
Lonely pyramids in the sand
All await
The red carpet debut,
Dawn of thoughtfulness,
Enlightenment rising from global
Wasteland ashes,
A sculpting in consciousness
Of concepts like laying down arms,
Creating livable environments,
Fostering long-lasting peace on
This third planet from the sun,
Presumed star-pupil of the solar system

The Laying of Hands

After the cutting,
After the slide under the microscope,
The herringbone stitches to the open flesh come

In a dutiful, meticulous sewing
Of the cancer-vacated crater in my temple,
Hybrid birth-child now of Nature and surgeon's handiwork

Setting as right as possible all that had gone
So terribly wrong in a matter of mere decades,
Now hand-stitched and shiny like a fine, leather shoe.

Basilica circa 2000 A.D.

A tarnished copper dome, expertly fitted
Over steel and concrete shell sheltering
Inside the ornate masterpiece of
The finest carved marble,
Exquisitely crafted wooden pews,
Polished sandstone and chiseled granite,
Richly colored murals with
Golden trim from the gilded strokes
Of master painters,
Saintly stories in stained glass
Painstakingly cut and welded with
Lead frame into whole form
By yet other Old World artisans whose
Creation, nourished by decades of
Pious devotion and religion-inspired generosity,
Rises defiantly into the new millennium
Above urban decay, gang-bangers
And people searching for their
Next food pantry.

Crawl

It is
tossed and tucked
into stone crevices, rolled
into plutonium dust and clay,
hidden, faded from view but not
memory.
It is
high endeavor, a song
persistent and soothing like
sea waves, like snowed over forests.
Search, search it out,
rappel the rock face, plow
the dust with determined hands,
uncover there the grail-like
essence of veritas
in hiding.

On a Hot Afternoon in Jerusalem

The sun-parched face of an old Arab
crowned with a kaffiyeh,
his nicotine-stained fingers clutching
a smoking Gauloise,
peers directly at the
photographer.
Is this a survivor of untold losses,
of so many blood-curdling mourning wails
of Arab women,
this very same man who sips black coffee
sugared to taste from a demitasse,
a sweet companion to his cigarette,
a sure soothing balm for desperate souls
in such toxic, war-torn environments,
here during a sweltering afternoon in the
calmer, narrow lanes of a Jerusalem souk
where Arabic words dance between
walls, then flee, muted, into the open air?
Does he dream too—that Allah
will some day silence
gunfire forever?

The Meaning of It

The sudden, unexpected parting of
The woman's lips into a smile, her
Face a flower in bloom, catches me
Off-guard, off my center of gravity
And sends me into an almost
Out-of-control spin of imagination that
Instinctively attempts to grasp the meaning of it,
Its reason for being the perversely wholesome
Intrusion that it is into the void of my solitude,
Tweaking in my consciousness that
Spark of curiosity that can only
Be felt in a heartbeat.

Oblivion

The antique statue of Sweet Jesus in the window—
One of mere wood and Colonial-era paint and decorated white
gown—
Must have teetered a little when
The ponytailed, blond twenty-something gringa
Came bouncing by on her all terrain three-wheeler
All decked-out in short shorts, sleeveless t-shirt, her
Queen of the road haughtiness lending the impression
That she was a mobile, better-watch-out-girl with
Cash to spare and a gleeful disregard for the
Pedestrians on the cobblestone streets of this
Mountainside town with soul-filling sunsets,
A Mexican colonial heritage to be inspired by,
A land of expats, sojourns with Cantinflas, the demise
Of Neal Cassady, the magnet that
Attracted some of Mexico's and the world's best artists.

La Americana did not see the faces of the indigenous and mestizo
Descendants of a once great Chichimec civilization.
She was oblivious to the secrets
In their eyes—the dried-up hope there—
Sowed by a succession of Spanish conquistadors,
Raging poverty, narco-traficantes in hopped-up Humvees,

And now, she of the three-wheeled vehicle
Scattering like chickens the pedestrians in her path as
Poor sweet Jesus delivers with tilted head
His characteristic, agonized bow of a Savior's forgiveness
From that window alongside
The cobbled lane.

The Myth of Red in Amsterdam

Women for hire in Amsterdam stand
in picture-windowed cells
lit up by red light that makes their
bikini panties and Victoria Secret lace bras glow
phosphorescently
creating a high sci-fi Barbarella look
for these beautiful exotic exiles who
come from distant locales, their fantasies
of Amsterdam really only a conduit into a
claustrophobic existence,
tutored by those in-the-know,
tutored by those in-the-know to coldly cut to the
bottom line while shrouded in soft red light, the
perfect milieu of predators and victims.
Here they await their metamorphosis into the
passionate, painted vixens they are presumed to be,
all in keeping with the age-old woman of the
night/john/pimp
dance of lust.
Great irony is in the air here.
Raucous carpe diem notions are mysteriously
muted and tamed.
I wonder if they see the tear in the corner
of my eye as I walk by.

Song of Graffiti

It is like fresh flowers lovingly placed in a vase,
Like free art for an otherwise dull, dreary wall,
Like a Japanese garden with raked gravel around
Carefully situated stones, like
A blues riff on a saxophone—
It is placed where crime, grit & poverty
Rise up like Medusa's snaky locks
In untold ways in seedy tenements where
Things are spawned every which way but up.
Graffiti brightens gray steel slabs on trains & walls
In otherwise sad-faced neighborhoods,
Rides in like a hero, a savior for those stepped on by
Capitalist dreams & Horatio Alger
Nightmares. Here's where bold blue swirls
With red & black out-lined John & Jane Doe figures,
Stylized gang tag signatures, yellow & green
& purple geometric strokes create a
Most glorious song of the dead rising
From the ashes.

Detour

Driving home that day
On the bleak, otherwise
Deserted road,
The man, trance-like,
Remembered deep green forests,
The picnic-worthy riverside
That was ever so pleasant with
Warm human touch, shared drink
And food, laughter—afternoons
Since lived and forgotten

By the aging man, now
On this isolated road across
His glaring current reality,
Across this path not of his choosing,
Not really sure where he's heading

In what seems like time-travel so
Distanced from those memories that
He now feels courted by
A siren, seductively singing from
The other side of his river memory,
A call to go to that river's edge and
Slide into its cool embrace, Zen-like,
Not pushing the water at all,
His fingers open-webbed like those of
A fetus free-floating in the womb.

Distraction

The ache that springs forth,
A jack-in-the-box pain, and you don't
Know its secret mission in your life—
The odds of guessing are best summarized by
Forget it, don't try, only force a grin
And concoct your notion of a peaceful
Island somewhere south of Cuba, nestled,
Only a dot in that Caribbean archipelago
Where perhaps you can get back in touch
With the serenity that you once knew
When you floated in the micro-sea of
Your mother's womb—What? you say, an event I
Don't remember, so you think instead of the
Soothing color emerald glimpsed in that magical island's
flora,
Maybe gemstone that is buried as deep as that aching
Inside of you, treasures both—body and gem cavern
In the empyrean.

The Special Hunter

A child-hunter alone in a shaded forest,
armed with a BB gun, embraces
otherwise alien, primitive instincts
not for survival, but out of sheer fascination
with scores of beautifully colored orioles,
cardinals, robins, blue jays & finches,
many of which will become fatalities,
trophies for the curious fantasies of
a boy-child-would-be-sharpshooter who
will simply palm each exquisite, avian corpse to
admire, with childlike wonder, its magnificent feathers,
beak curvature, and its evolutionary physiology.
At best, it is murder for beauty, with
innocence abounding, but
oh, so lethal.

A Story to Tell

There was something in the man's tone of voice,
something between bittersweet and sad and perhaps
matter-of-factness as he related the days when he was
on the same billing as Hendrix, his profound love for
the star's genius, his recognition of how much that icon
helped him to develop a bluesy rock style of his own,
and how much he now misses playing gigs
at some of the smoky, beer-bottle-littered joints where
his own music once rocked . . . but those were
the good old golden times that reside in pure
time frozen in space, like silent
blue stars, the kind that hang delicately
in conversational moments like those,
underneath which the fragile dream
of spotlights shone around him again.

Desert Walk

My feet crunch
the crust of this place.
Imagination conjures up
curious thoughts
about this soil's substance:
dinosaur fossil chunks,
Native American pottery parts,
broken rattlesnake fangs,
crystallized, baked
sea sediments
All here on this moon-like
surface.

I look to the real moon in the
pale-blue afternoon sky above,
wondering if there
I would be
one step closer to Heaven.

This place can chill you
or burn you up
with its dry, icy, sometimes hot
breath --this desert.

Here life and death
are separated by a
very thin line
over the millennia.

Copper Dream

This is really Neruda's land,
land of campesinos, rotos, Chile Mierda,
land of Salvador Allende's spaghetti Western fantasies
of good versus evil amid shadows of gray,
lightness and darkness,
land where social contrast triumphs over social justice.
Clint Eastwood has no idea that he was
a hero of the first freely elected Marxist leader
in Latin America, the man who would be
one among many of the victims
of Pinochet's slick-holstered Boys.
The dream of Neruda's land
remains connected to me by a thin thread
spun out of dusty memories of my alien status there,
in the land of campesinos, rotos, and
Chile Mierda.

A View from Above

There are times
when you can
touch the sky
at 16,000 feet
by raising your
arm high &
letting the icy bite
of mountain air
anesthetize
your fingertips,
here
above everything
below this gray Andean peak
here
in the white cotton clouds
that intermittently enshroud
the blue heavens above, the
craggy rock & the timberline
vegetation clear down to the
ground zero din of everyday Earth struggle,
here
where your lungs,
your body & mind
lust for air,
strain & dream
of easy breath —
pay the price
for
the beauty of it all.

The Miracle

The walk to the bus stop, then the two buses
To the place weren't all that bad—no obstacle, really.
His mind on hold until he gets there,
To the clinic he's chosen, call it
A raw pilgrimage for it is there he will go
Deep-water today, down among the ice-fish,
The albino sharks, the quivering eels of his soul
 In dark, deep depths whose pressure will contort his face
Into that of the beast that lurks inside,
His reservoir of hatred and anguish is like
Molten lava beginning to overflow,
A pressure unstoppable as he
Morphs into that other person he has met in the past.
There is thunder in the sky, a lightning bolt or two,
As he walks toward the clinic—just a few more steps
And he will become the wolf inside whose howls
Will rattle the walls there, releasing again
Beggar Lazarus to be raised from the dead—
Freed from his overwhelming disquiet
Until his demons push him back again.

Blocked

Just beyond the sandy crest
Dates bake in the sun,
Water is poured into tin drums,
Children watch their fathers
Stroll away down roadsides.

And those children, bursting
Inside with angels and demons,
Wonder about slingshot throws,
Feel impervious to real bullets,
The threat of demolition by
Bulldozer, soldiers who think
Of them as animals—each side
Out of touch with their Semitic
Muscle fiber, their similar genetic
Codes, despite the different paths
They have taken to the same place.

Each other's sweat is not seen.
Each other's blood is not seen.
Each other's life is not seen.
Each other's family is not seen.

There is only blindness, at times
Blistered by the sun, at times
Chilled by cool and rainy winters with
Rivulets of water inhaled by the waiting
Parched earth.

II.

In Style

I've seen them all along: the needy, statuesque figures with fingers curled, the solitary people except for the others like them, the ones with the same addiction, pariahs in their own right, they stand, a quick gaze here or there at other passers-by, at cars that speed by, at glassed-in buildings even on the coldest and the hottest days. There they are sustained by their hits, as smoke billows from their lips during their legally-imposed sojourns, their acts of compliant isolation cheered on by the ghost of the Marlboro Man. To those in the clouds among us, death by smoke is gusto-seeking, macho, sexy-cool. The unwitting Bogart and Bacall oozed the seductive amalgam of sex and smoke and the public swooned; Cooper, Lana Turner, Nat King Cole and Billie-who-sang-the-blues were all victims of the fashionable trends concocted by admen clever enough to sell fate in cellophane-covered, colorful packs of good life allure.

Flight 006

I did not really believe the stick-thin porteño seated next to me on the flight from Santiago to Buenos Aires when he leaned into me with an elbow-tap and voluntarily confessed that, in all his years as an air traffic controller, only once did he experience a UFO, one that five months before had hovered above the glass tower of the main airport in Buenos Aires for what seemed like a frozen minute before shooting a laser-like beam that cleanly pierced the glass tower just seconds before it flew off and became instantly invisible. I noticed the peculiar way the man with the pencil-line mustache nodded as he narrated his tale, as though he were trying to convince himself of what he had just related. After all, grabbing a stranger on a plane to tell all that to was, I thought, marginally bizarre if not downright so. And to add to the strangeness, we later parted with just a handshake as we exited the plane in the land of the porteños.

This life is undeniably full of enigmas, not to mention quirky people, so flake is the word- impression I had as I glanced across the carousel as he appeared to be in a deep state of impenetrable thought, oblivious to everyone and everything around him. I retrieved my bag and exited through Customs never to see the man again.

As plagued as I was at the time by what might be described as the Peace Corps Volunteer wanderlust syndrome, I arrived about two weeks later in Buenos Aires after my travels up to Uruguay and Brazil with just about enough money to pay for a flight over to Mendoza, just over the Andes from Chile where I needed to return like three days before. It turned out that there happened to be a U.S. Air

Force base there where two pilots adopted this feckless wayfarer for three days before paying for a taxi-van up over the Andes to Santiago. As they were driving me to the taxi, I related the story about the man on the plane, and, as I was doing so, they looked at each other and grinned. They both flew "missions" over South America, and they seemed to know of what I spoke.

The Signal

A five hour road trip and three hours of moving my daughter
back into her dormitory have left me hot and tired, a refugee in
a downtown Minneapolis hotel. Nevertheless, I feel obliged to call
an elderly aunt whom I have seen a total of four times over the last
quarter century. When she answers, her reedy voice quavers with
a peculiar tone of strident urgency, and she asks . . . no, she
insists that we drive out to visit her and my uncle at their west-side
suburb, really the last thing on my mind this humid, smoldering
late-summer afternoon with threatening-looking storm clouds
already thundering across the plains off to the west. So I
regrettably decline her frantic request and tell her that such a trip
would be nigh on impossible, which is something that my aunt
does not want to hear because she obsessively repeats her wish
with her former urgency now turned to a tone of sheer desperation.
A captive of exhaustion, I do not take the hint, nor can I hear her
real message, the one vibrating up from her heart like a call from
the other world to which only she knows she will soon go.

Baton

On a grassy rise adjacent to a footbridge, small children speckle
the spring grass during a short respite from their classroom, some
rolling full speed with arms flailing every which way—some with
cautious, almost deliberate half and full turns while, above on the
knoll, some women, mere shadows against the sky behind, watch
over them. They look from child to child as each child navigates
the slope. Chances are they are not as wont to pay too much
attention to the willy-nilly rollers who, with their oxygen rush, will
not get injured, much like drunken drivers who sustain only minor
injuries if any. Instead, it's the slow rollers, the overly careful ones
who are red-flagged by the attending adults because they are the
ones who are injured the most, their little uptight twists and turns
predisposing them to broken bones, ankle sprains, a clobbering or
two from collisions with the willy-nilly ones who flatten them on
contact because of their wild abandon. Just how much the flagged
ones will learn without their caretakers' advice becomes part of the
myriad choices parents must face as they sculpt and mold their
loved ones into the adults that will someday tower over them in
life, and watch them in return, lovingly, thoughtfully in their
circular dance.

Epitaph on a Late-Winter Mouse

One evening, my younger daughter, with
just a tinge of hysteria, brought to my attention
what appeared to be a strange, dancing mouse cavorting
about on the maple floorboards of our kitchen, a veritable
Nureyev of his species, one full of energy or spunk or maybe
just crazy as hell. He seemed, she said, to be
executing pirouettes & solo leaps. To rule out
hallucinations on my daughter's part, I set
mousetraps that very evening.

The next morning, I stood over the carcass of
a mouse covered from his mid-section
and above by the wooden plank of the mousetrap
which left visible only the tan fur of his belly,
hind legs, & a tail as straight as a marsh reed.

I reached down and flipped over the trap only
to find myself face-to-face with the creature, his
tiny jet-black eyes looking up at me, almost
accusingly, as if I were a Goliath-like henchman
who, with unmistakable malevolent intention, had
put an end to his very successful
dancing career.

On an Otherwise Sunny Day

One day the doves couldn't take it anymore, so they converged from all parts of the USA over Kansas City, causing considerable alarm among air traffic controllers across the country, shutting down flights everywhere. Then, without the slightest hint, they flew vertically in one massive cloud that darkened the entire state of Kansas on what had been a gloriously sunny day, an event that paralyzed onlookers in their tracks, caused mouths to gape open, and some people shouted "Oh, my god!" (or some variation thereof) which echoed throughout the gathered throngs. Meanwhile, the doves formed an almost perfect circle of specks, and winged up into the heavens!

Sadly, no one saw or heard from a single dove again—The species had vanished. Only rumors abounded: That the doves found a new home in the rings of Saturn, that they had inhabited the Moon, formed colonies on Mars—even that they were only bent-on suicide and flew into the Sun's corona, perishing there forever. That they found a different orb is open to conjecture, and at best is but a surreal event frozen now in infinite space.

Falling to Heaven

One of life's little tricks guided me up my basement stairs,
my hands loaded with three bottles of wine from the cellar
for thirsty guests at a dinner party. As it turned out, the trick
was a clumsy stumble, my right shoe jamming into something on
the steps, sending me sprawling forward helplessly, hands full,
unable to brake my lunge toward the top few steps, alas, making
my right knee slam into the edge of one of them. Ergo pain,
humiliation, a lingering assessment of life, human
vulnerability, Fate's wishes, and, oh yes, Heaven.

If there is a Heaven, and I should be so fortunate to reach it
someday—perhaps after a more serious tumble—what would it be
like? Would I gain entry on probation for three to six months, or
would I be a model angel in the place, much to the envy of others
there? The place being Heaven, would I take on a persona other
than a knotty-kneed, increasingly accident-prone shuffler, or would
I assume a Nureyevian gracefulness that would readily distinguish
me from other less agile angels?

What's more, it's probably a safe assumption that, in Heaven, there
are no basement stairs to scale, fewer, if any, traps for innocent
souls like me to be snared by, houses of clouds ever so soft to the
touch that bruises are downright impossible, where top-notch pinot
noir is just a wink away.

The Chair

On an autumn afternoon my wife settles in the padded cherry wood chair in the corner of our dining room just in time for the sun's rays to paint her and the chair with a golden hue and warmth. I glance at her as I pass by on my way upstairs to the study. She is often drawn to this chair, the one that has comforted relatives on my father's Norwegian side for a couple of centuries.

We don't know who made this chair with its firm, sturdy frame. Perhaps my great-great grandfather in Oslo or Gran in Oppland Fylke or Pukerud made it sometime before the journey to this new land in 1849. The chair survived the transatlantic voyage, but I imagine it cootie-infested, rat-nested in the hold of their ship, the Flora. Once ashore, the chairtraveled to the Midwest.

Our Norwegian heirloom chair with its hand-carved details has seen many types of padding and upholstery. It outlived three generations of my family, comforted dozens, and it still welcomes anyone seeking repose or a special place amidst all of our modern store-bought belongings. Our chair's only demand is that someone like my wife will, with tolerance for its antiquity, keep it company from time to time.

Westward

In Norway, this country lane winds through barley fields,
and down rolling hills with a large lake and surrounding
forests that skirt sister churches that stand like stone barns,
like village sergeants guarding farms
from trolls, blight and other forms of harmful
lore in these post-Viking parts forgotten
long ago by those who fled this charmed place—
pilgrims charged with a westward voyage.

The Place They Never Forgot

The rotating barber's pole lured those seeking a haircut into Hank's place, but so did his legendary fame as the best barber in his neighborhood. Veteran customers knew better than to expect what you might typically regard as a barber full of friendly repartee or child-friendly comments—Hank was gruff, a grumbler at best, and seemed to live in the world of opera solos from Verdi's La Traviata,Aida, and Bizet's Carmen that serenaded him and his customers, sometimes in scratchy renditions of their godliness that echoed from an old phonograph atop a nearby table. It might be a reasonable assumption that Hank generated many future opera lovers (or haters) as a result, and that most, if not everyone, loved, or at least, respected him. He did it Hank's way — bare bones, no frills, and he gave you what you really entered his shop for. When you left Hank's domain, with your neck powdered and your hair freshly-clipped, groomed and with that famous "a little dab'll do ya" stuff, one could not help but feel like a recruit given reprieve to exit again into the glare of the afternoon sun, ready for the onslaught of crazed girls who couldn't wait "to get their hands into your excitingly clean, disturbingly healthy hair now so full of life" — until shagginess would again give you your marching orders back to Hank's place.

The Jingle Song on the Train Home

The temperature and humidity on that sweltering
summer night was steam-bath grade on the train
into which scores of jubilant Yankee fans poured
into its wall-to-wall soup following a defeat of the Red Sox.

Amidst the chatter between passengers
a few minutes into the sweatbox no a.c. ride,
a voice hovered above the din at our end of the carriage. Like
most rogue buskers, the woman was perceived as yet another
petty annoyance exercising her impromptu
venue rights, there with plastic cup in hand, she
launched into an a Capella rendition of "Lean on Me."

But then, something magical happened when
her singing began, little by little, to infiltrate
passengers' awareness, and drew some with
her gripping, sorrowful spirit to clap in rhythm and to sing
along with words like " . . . we all need somebody to lean on."

Now, granted, she was no Ma Rainey, but the duende
lurked there in her presentation to the extent that some
were ready to donate spare change to her, but I, deep
in conversation, had none, so the best I could do was to smile
and nod my appreciation (or was it sympathy?) as she glanced
my way when she walked by.

Passing down the aisle, the toothless woman sang on
before exiting with a smile of appreciation, her cup far from full
as she shuffled on to the next car.

Could it be that something, just something might be all right
for her   somewhere at the end of the line?

On the Road to Mayo

The road itself across Wisconsin, then the western banks of the
Mississippi River consoled us—we took back roads—a scenic,
snail-paced journey devoid of numbing interstate rushing and bug-
spattered windshield. Mick Jagger rocked us with Satisfaction
while we both took in the sights on the winding drive along the
river, going north on the Iowa and Minnesota sides, stopping
briefly to watch a bald eagle glide into a majestic dive to snatch a
fish from the water. The riverside bluffs on both sides loomed like
stoic, timeless guardians of the river treasure flowing below. We
stopped to admire prairie flowers a little farther up the winding
road, crossed the flat, black-earthed Minnesota farm fields and
drove on through the rolling prairie land until we finally entered
Rochester city limits. Famished, we found a roadside café where
we prided ourselves in ordering and devouring greasy
cheeseburgers and sipped malted shakes, just like we did when
we were love-struck grad students many moons ago. I
couldn't resist the old juke box there so I slipped two quarters in
the slot. As Jagger sang *You Can't Always Get What You Want,* in
the distance we could see Mayo Clinic puncturing the late
afternoon sky, a place full of busy magiciansin that Mecca of hope,
now shimmering in that ever so reachable distance before us.

A Comic Cover Riddle

Breaking news: A young, completely bald boy dressed in a red T-shirt, matching red socks and black shorts was seen grasping a sleeping man's right arm with both hands, an act that could have awakened the snoring man in a start and prompted him to yell at the boy who would not have been totally surprised by the man's anger, and would have attempted to justify his presumed aggression with the man's floppy arm by explaining that all he was trying to do was to spare the man of having the fly buzzing around his head land on him, and, such being the boy's intention, he was acting altruistically albeit perhaps not wisely because he would have — had he had complete follow-through — either shooed the fly away using the man's own hand or, at worst, inadvertently squashed the fly on top of the man's ever-so-vulnerable head.

Wait a minute: truth be told, this is really comic book fiction created by my great uncle, Carl Anderson, who, in a moment of artistic license about a half century ago, dreamed up the above cover for his Dell comic book series called "Henry" (circa 1948), one that sold for a fancy 10 cents.

It should be noted that, to this day, the above cover has piqued the curiosity of philosophers, psychologists, comic book connoisseurs and sundry other people whose diverse takes go round and round and rarely intersect.

And in the shadows of past art, an innocent dances before the gawkers..

Reminiscence on a Sunday Afternoon

One sunny fall afternoon I, a man with no name, step out onto the deck to relax. It is an exceptionally quiet day, except for the birds that begin their birdsong without hesitation. I become their audience. After an unknown time there in my trance-like state, I realize that my coming out today was purpose-driven, that my left hand still clutches the garage door opener I had picked up on the way out. I give it a click. As the door opens grindingly, it does so with a screeching sound reminiscent of, as best as I can tell, Ennio Morricone's score for The Good, the Bad and the Ugly; I am suddenly under the rich blue Almerian sky in Spain where Sergio Leone cranked out that Spaghetti western circa 1966. Silence...no bird song. Just a man with no name now transported to the mesquite-covered plains of Almeria, dressed in cowboy garb atop my stallion next to another pale-faced rider—Clint Eastwood— who, with piercing blue eyes and a small cigar between his lips, glances over at this man with no name and says, "Sorry mister, I got to get going...You coming with?" For unknown reasons, I stay put as Clint rides off down the dusty road, his six-shooter's blue metal glistening under the Spanish sun. Black out...return to my backyard birdsong, I with no name am seated exactly where I was before, garage opener in hand. The uncertain fate of my garage door is seriously pondered. I pause a moment, but then I click the opener impulsively, so I can hear Morricone at least one more time.

Rome, July 2012

In the crowds, J. Caesar is invisible. He walks the streets of Rome
as a shadow of himself, wades in the cool waters of the Trevi
Fountain but does not make a ripple, reads the commemorative
plaque outside the door to Keat's house at the foot of the Spanish
Steps, listens to open-air chamber concerts in the Jewish Quarter
near the Octavian Gate. He watches the feral cats in flagrante
delicto where his blood was spilled by Brutus and his co-
conspirators in the Roman Senate, now a lackluster, hard-to-find
patch of weed, sand and crumbling stone. On Sunday afternoons, J.
Caesar is drawn to the Colosseum, Vespasian's major opus; there,
on the upper tier, he reviews the stone skeleton of what once was.
At times like these, he wonders if fate could have been something
different. Brutus, oh most contemptible Brutus! On Rome's many
streets, Brutus' specter haunts him until one humid day when J.
Caesar takes refuge in the Sistine Chapel where, among the works
of Michelangelo, he thinks he sees Brutus in the horrified face of
the man whom Jesus is casting to a devil in Hell. A smile erupts on
Caesar's face, you know, the would-have-been Rex of the Roman
Empire were it not for Brutus, all for the justice and deliverance
found in one of Michelangelo's frescoes—Where else but in
modern Rome on a hot, very hot summer day.

Concurrence

Someone asks me what place I've enjoyed living in
during my life of travels
& I say—after some deliberation—
A place is a place is a place is a place &
People are people are people no matter
Where you are.
& the other then says, Aren't people different
in the different places you find them? & I say
people are basically the same at their core
wherever you go.
& she then asks, But don't people define their locale? to which
I respond that they do only superficially by some environmental
& cultural whitewash that covers their basic core.

I then ponder whether the American river I'm standing by is
The same as the Seine, the Thames, the Volga, the Blue Danube....
& I conclude that a river is a river is a river with its
murky water flowing endlessly, lapping its walled shores
with its toxic soup that invites only those
with what Virginia Woolf had in mind in perhaps a different,
more desperate, but possibly same quandary.

Compass

Here I am encapsulated in one of those dreams,
although nightmare might be a better name for it.
I ride the subway, get off, and reenter the next train,
wonder if I'm on the right subway: Is It the "G" or
the "F" train I should be on? Which stop will get me
to where I think I should be going? This goes on until I conclude
that I'm really lost and rudderless in this sea of people,
all of whom seem to know exactly where they are in this
particular place and time in this staggering city
where sunsets hide behind concrete skyscrapers,
this place where even Freud would have had a nervous
breakdown had he the courage to come here and sit
next to me on this subway without any idea of where his
executive function would/could take him. No, he wouldn't have
had the balls to ask the young Asian woman seated next to him
for directions when his emotions were starting to spew
and flood his brain with norepinephrine and cortisol ,
until that empathetic woman administers to the clueless,
pathetic man some compass points with which he just might
navigate a course to the place for which he thinks he is bound,
where people are nervously considering his fate.

The List

Now dear, do not forget to pick up the following: 1 1/2 lb. of chicken pieces, 2 cans of coconut milk (so much rides on this ingredient!), a small bottle of extra virgin olive oil (just virgin will simply not do!), one Vidalia onion, at least two garlic cloves, 2 packs of fresh pigeon peas (you'd be a DREAM if you could only find the Trinidadian one!), 2 pimiento peppers (not jalapeños and not Scotch bonnet), 10-12 juicy limes and 1/2 lb. of chorizo sausage. Sweetheart, I could have used these things about 2 hours ago, but do your best, okay?

So after 53 minutes of store time in no less than a total of five stores, I arrive home with the above ingredients, panting as I lug the bags in, and she sighs in one of those Oh-my-God-I-can't-believe-that-I-forgot-to-tell-you to pick up 2 bottles of Trinidadian 10 Cane rum! No sooner than she has uttered the last word of that regrettable statement than I am walking to the corner liquor store, a neighborhood adventure — well at least a walk with what most probably will hold some cardiovascular benefit for this man of errands. I have always admired and loved to view the idiosyncratic architecture of our area.

III.

The House Alongside

When I was a seven-year-old cowboy
sitting on a rented-by-the-hour palomino pony,
I grinned, expectantly waiting
for the photo-snap that would record
for posterity, me, the bare-chested boy
sweating in the Georgia summertime sun,
with holstered revolvers, a cowboy
hat, bandanna & even cowhide chaps.
I smiled for the camera with
a cherub's freckled face, hiding
well, I'm sure, the mischievous
soul of a boy given so much privilege.

Now, looking at that image on
what has become a faded
yellowy picture, I wonder at
how easy it was for me then
to suspend so magically my awareness
of my mother who lay dying in the red
brick house that so magnificently
framed us—my fantasy
palomino pony & me.

Swing with Chains

It is clear it was swung low, and high at times
in arcs, a fun pendulum in magical air. Not

understood in children's short-term
memories was the intent behind each push.

Instead, those august moments are now
erased by rotting swing seat now dangling

from rusty chains, belying the mist of love
still hovering there under

the gentle shade of the elm.

Missing

for Nani

The mind goes wild
Wondering why a thin,
Delicate young woman
Becomes convinced that
She can immerse her
Sari-clad self in the Atlantic
And swim back to her native India,
Back to an abject poverty
That has not yet defined itself
In this newly found land,
Island in the tropics,
Mecca for indentured immigrants like her
Just ten degrees north of the equator, a
Stones throw from Tobago,
Or Venezuela, or Grenada,
Back to that from which she ran
Fickle-hearted to start,
Now to perish in her primitive desire,
Cleansed and swallowed by
The relentless waves of the
Unforgiving, blue sea.

The Lament

From shadows jackals come,
their clenched teeth jagged
with sure bite on my friend's flesh.
There is no remorse
in their wild, black eyes.
No thought, no consideration for my
stinging loss--no chance for reprieve
from their locked-shut judgment.

If I could only tell them
how much my friend is valued;
if they could only listen
to my a cappella song,
here in the day's deep
darkness.

Jewel

One early morning
A neonatal messenger from another world
Caught my eye with the twinkle in his.

Angelic there, swathed in white linens and knitted cap,
He spoke to me in a wordless language,
Real on a plane beyond

Normal human discourse, a pipeline
From the mysterious forces out there,
Here, offering in all his innocence

The wisdom, perhaps the grail, we all
Secretly seek as daytime trippers and
Nighttime dreamers imagining

Diamond-glitter like this.

Reverie

The stars—
the very same ones
beheld by
my wide-eyed ancestors in the early 1800s—
now shine on me, brightly as they did then
in the Midwestern north country where
those spirited relatives built sod-houses on their tracts of land
with rough hands and sheer
determination, not too far from where I,
some time and distance apart,
sit watching Shakespeare
under that same canopy of stars,
a smile of wonder on my face while caught up in
A Midsummer Night's Dream,
the cicada serenade,
the late summer cool caress of night air—

a communion with an apartness
not really understood there . . .

On the Edge of the World

If only …
If I could have only talked
About my dreams as easily as
Simply greeting you. If only I
Could have nurtured your gifts to
Me as one cares for a plant seedling,
Or, standing on the edge of the World,
Like a true lover of stars shimmering so
Delicately in all the blackness around, seen
Your radiant light, kissed its lips in an embrace.

These could-haves have moved on and
Become bones buried in the desert sand,
Then exposed by erosion force, sun-bleached
And powdered by the wind, spread like
Dust somewhere into the horizon and
Reclaimed by time.

Sub-Tropicana

You have become the North American glamour queen,
Mecca of south coast breezes, imbiber of
Rum punch,
Mojitos,
Brewer of cortaditos &
Occasional cafés con leche,
You seduced & forged glass,
Concrete & steel into
Modern skylines
& blended it with older art deco
Renovations along South Beach
Salsa beats that you sent
Dancing, spinning right down to
The waves off the blue Atlantic &
South along cold cut sea-sprayed
Skyscraper glass & then over the waves
Clear out to Cuba/Cuba,
Inviting, enticing determined balseros with rumors
Of greener grass in places like Little Havana,
Home of hands wide open for money flying in
With affluent Latinos, Europeans, an open
Port for asylum-seekers of all stripes to
Come to this gyrating, buzzing Latin beat
That is this Cosmopolis (with capital "C")
Retrofitted in pastels & neon, lover of
Blurred identities.

Things Said

Can anesthetize the tongue,
Create musical metaphor,
Cajole,
Burn a soul like a hot poker iron,

Kindle love in a lover's heart like
The music from a Gypsy's violin,

Stoke a war and, later,
Entreat peace,

Project blame, admit past sins,
Turn around a life teetering on
The edge of despair,

Raise a child from newborn—
Mentor a new spirit.

Legacy

No easy task this
Cleanup of basement workbench
Full of multifarious clutter,
Dusty mementos of hand-me-downs.
The real chore is in tossing the
Handmade tools my father
Crafted as a machinist under
The final shadows of WW II
And the scraped-up pale-blue tackle box
Full of Lazy Ikes, Bombers, Jitterbugs,
River Runt Spooks, and
Hula Poppers.
A simple matter on the surface
But what's not seen is
The slippery thought of
Letting go of steel craft and memories,
Lovingly bequeathed as if
They were brothers whose being
I'm now releasing like unwanted
Fish, letting them drop from my hands
To the trash bin below, letting them go
While I suppress a traitor's smile,
Great Judas at the workbench, son
Who is not much more than an ingrate
Who will probably keep only the tackle box
In the end.

A Trip to That Place

Now we glide into that placeth . . . at
town, no, now that city last experienced
decades ago. Then a child, now an adult
driving myself towards something now
so abstract: places, people—town-city-people
transformation—only yet to define itself
for this errant, solitary traveler in exile
from this place—whole lives,
births, deaths . . . long after the fact, mere
notices in the paper ever so far
from those quieted souls who were once
family, now nothing but tombstones to
greet those like me on silent grassy knolls.

A Gift of Lavender

A beautifully potted lavender plant, a
gift from a poet-friend,
has begun to wilt & turn color,
despite our good attention & untutored
nurturing, like the mysterious
disconnect that sometimes occurs
between a leukemia patient
and his nurse. It has begun to march
to a strange, unseen drummer, much to
our great sadness & sense of
loss, prompting us to prepare ourselves
for a unique, very special
bereavement.

We have planned a decent burial for
it in our backyard next to our hearty
rose of Sharon tree. We hope that
the tree's roots will savor the
lavender plant's delicate, recycled
company, a wedding, we think, that
will breed an irresistible lavender
Hibiscus brandy, a sure-fire elixir
for the honeybees next mid-summer.

Free Fall

The girl was accused
the cause of her past

as if as a child she were
person enough

to wreck in a tempest
the family ship

and thereby end any happiness
residing therein—

as if, solo, she could navigate so,
and, sorcerer-like, cast stars

in that universe

as if she were monster-made,
not just a young spirit

trapped in a black hole vacuum
of nonrecognition—

but spawned from Creator's magic web,
an angel ripe with promise

now bound for only a pirouette
on a vanishing cloud

above her bleak landscape.

On the Glade Near Strawberry Fields

We huddled and cried together,
looking up at the moon
on a starry, autumn night.

We prayed with frantic but
unquestionable devotion to
a God who seemed, in the end,
not to hear.

We held hands in a field of
leaf-shrouded grass while birds sang
their irrepressible bird songs.
And nothing changed.

Now, we have grown hoarse
from suppressed screams
that now only find outlet in
repetitive, guttural intonations
as we keep asking why and go on
imagining.

On Stargazing

Today I wash my hands
as if to insure a clean tender touch
as if to scramble or nullify
any coup against the image
of fresh life flower held and so coveted
   in secret moments
during dawn breaking the night
as if paper can be saved from fire
as if I can tilt at misunderstood
windmills without a less romantic better half
as if answers come with Sisyphean effort
as if the sounds of solitude will calm me
as if forever . . .

Channel Changer

I. Weather Report—

Hell no! You say the wind is too damned strong
But I say I rather like the ride it gives the waves
And its boldness with trees prone to be sassy to it.
I like its resoluteness, even its hurricane force on
Those often defiant shores populated by stilted homes
That are forever thumbing their nose at its will.

II. The Oldie but Goodie TV Reruns—

Watching the Lone Ranger on tv as a child magically
Catapulted me into fantasies about him leaving Tonto,
And pairing up with Dale Evans as his side-kick—
Or whatever, the consequence of which would have left
Gene Autry with a transformative Native American partner,
Which might have been a small step for mankind at

The time, but innovative at the same time. It is encouraging
To imagine that Gene would have maybe devised a
New name for the ever tolerant and humble Tonto—
Something less demeaning than his screen name which
Means "stupid" in Spanish, truly inappropriate for what
He really was—a savvy and loyal pal to his bipolar friend

On his steed, Silver. Let's dub him with something more
Noble like Golden Eagle or Eknath (poet) or hell, even
Tarak(Star), you know, anything not so ignorantly demeaning
As goddamned Tonto for Christ's sake!

III. Et Cetera

And then, what if Lucy had left Ricardo and had run off with
Landlord Fred Mertz, and consequently left "Ricky"Ricardo
To Spirit-off and form a liaison with Ethel,
Thereby changing the Whole constellation of their worlds
And their respective offspring?
Or, in the Honeymooners, Trixie with Alice, or Ralph with both
Alice and Trixie? Or whatever, combinations that could have truly
Transformed tv . . .

Musings on a Wall

A horse depicted on a cave wall
by Paleolithic dwellers is dissected
by cracks coursing through it:
neck/head
chest/front legs
thorax/
back to tail/
hind quarters/,
all set against and bordered
by brown and ocher
and black ash tones
with a sun symbol somehow
lighting the darkness
there In cave shadows,
a refuge from the spirits
outside
A horse of value—
one to escape on
A ghost horse on which
to follow the sun
in tune with the altogether mashup
of tribal honor and beliefs
A symbol of survival
for redemption-seekers
in the cool, dark depths
there . . .

At the Oriental Theater in Milwaukee

Something tells me that the little man
in striped short sleeves and a Sears' tie
could really cut loose with a wild, wailing
boogie-woogie on that awesome Kimball concert organ
on stage down at the Oriental Theater,
instead of the take-me-out-to-the-ballgame/true-blue
schmaltz he is probably told to play before the previews
come on. Not that there's anything patently wrong
with his standard repertoire, but that magnificent organ
has got to be capable of so much more, as I'm sure the man is.

Watching him play, I can imagine him suddenly exploding
into a Ray Charles or, hell, even a Jerry Lee Lewis rocking
rendition in which he shakes the sleepy, popcorn-eating, soda
swilling place up a bit, maybe even bringing those exotic moldings
and fixtures to life before the main feature sparkles
from the screen.

And so, every time I'm sitting there waiting for the big screen fare,
I'll imagine how nice it would be if he could, just once,
snap out of the corral he's in, out of all that has been constrained
inside, and make hulk-like all that stuff barely breathing there.

On Fire in America

I am an American even if I'm from a town smaller than Topeka,
Or two hundred miles south of Sacramento,
From Red Hook in Brooklyn near the river,
Or north of there from the Bronx or Harlem or east toward Bed-
Stuy, A farm near Oshkosh near Oshkosh-By-Gosh,
From D.C., or Charleston or Memphis or from Tulsa,
A descendent of the massacred in Indian wars and urban riots
Across the land, Or of parents from other cultures around the
globe,
A child of the Rainbow, A Katrina victim, homeless/hopeless with
A tattered horizon, A tornado survivor scratching his head in
Alabama during elusive sunsets, A sandbagger holding back river-
Floodwaters in flood years, A card-carrying union member in
Union-busting states Turning tears into fuel for activism while
Watching home and livelihood evaporate at the whim
Of bottom-line autocrats high on the taste of killer-politics now
Epidemic in this land, this dream that has evolved into
A Darwinian land devoid of noblesse oblige,
A blood-spattered land, this mutant offspring
Of one fine original
Constitution.

Woodland Sojourn

—from *Woodgatherer* (Le Pere Jacques) 1881
                    by Jules Bastien-Lepage]

The old man does not pick
                    flowers . . . he
just looks for dried dead wood and then bears
                    his wood bundle with bent back.
Almost tottering over,
                    his eyes fixed in reverie on his next find, not
on his grand-daughter over whom he towers
                    while she, in blue dress, is drawn to
forest flowers. The old man, he wears earth tones
                    befitting his rural persona,
and seems ready to exit his life of toil, the one
                    now moving toward loading one last branch
                                        someday.
Does he do it all for the tiny
                    bouquet of freshly picked wildflowers
that the little girl in blue will hand to him?
                    The innocent smile,
                                        symbol
of future generations back home?

The Rebel Nymph

—from *Isadora Duncan*, 1911, by John Sloan

Isadora, the stage for you is a shadowy specter
Against which you, in pink flash, brighten the
Soul of all of us curious captives of your spirit
While we watch you dance in and out of the darkness
There, and pass in triumph, like the rebellious nymph
That you are, into backlit orange crescent slivers that
Defy the fate that seeks to destroy your spark
Of genius that gave you the gift to dance on,
With untold stars shining on you, lighting
The way to Modern Dance in our lives
Despite your tragic, iridescent silk scarf
That pulled you from us in one quick pluck.

On Meeting Again

How will I know you when
You return? I will tell you
What I imagine; then, you can
Either let the sun shine on me or
Eclipse me with the truth. I will

See you as the rain on my window,
The majestic juniper in my yard,
The calm-spirited lake bordered by
Those perfect maple, oak and
Pine trees at dawn,
When hope fires up
In my heart, to see you appear again
In front of me, within my
Reach, so that I can share what was so terribly
Unexpressed with you before you took the
Path least wanted and quietly exited into
The blackness of night on the back of the ghost stallion,
To join what beckoned you in your youth, maybe
To the caves there that no one can imagine, a
Place of soulful silence, the volumes of worlds.

Horizon

Above me birds are skittering
their sky trade

So smoothly—effortless
stark white actors in

relief against the canopy
of powder-blue sky

while I, with sad
humanoid hands,

am only
a serial onlooker,

a puppet at the podium
offering only this

Hurricane

The first clue the sky gives
is a slate-gray grimace, followed by
a sea-sprayed wind, coarse but cleansing
to the Earth's languorous perfume from flower and tree breaths.
Coconut clusters topping trees shake like maracas, a creaky
dance to now accelerated high-notch winds,
winds that threaten this island's
slow calypso beat, threaten to push it
to a salsa or even reguetón against its better cultural pull,
followed by a nightcap of sea surge that bathes
the island's sand, even where it had been virgin dry
since the last storm that gyrated over from the
African coast that named it outcast and leaper,
worthy only of the New World.

A Tribute to the Penguin-Men Among Us

who huddle around watching their young ones
take to the ice like the wobbly creatures they are
at outdoor school rinks now lent to these
bundled-up fathers who shift from side to side
and huddle together to stay warm like
looming Emperor Penguins,
while dutifully standing vigil for their
offspring who careen wildly but then
glide like pros for up-to-seconds-at-a-time before
spiraling into impromptu, shaky pirouettes
that cause the men to gasp from the sidelines,
then fake-skate with their shoes
over to the crash site where they whisper
their concern and, upon further triage,
encourage their fallen angels to right their little
skates on the ice, to again take on the
wintry reality of the late afternoon,
with their chins held high to the glory of
the Penguin-Men in attendance.

Beauty Hidden Within

For Alfred Sessler,1909-1963

The artist's studio was securely nested just
Off of the carved oak balustrade

Behind a door left locked to ward off
Curious spying souls from witnessing

The treasures within, those hidden and tucked
Along the walls for the most part with an

Occasional exception of segregated pieces
Of art that, for unknown reasons, had

Found the privilege of being centrally
Placed like lonesome islands declaring their

Own nationhood, special and different
From the others, in this kingdom of

Lithographs, this jungle portraying twisted
Tree trunks, contorted faces that were

Ugly at first glance, but which held a
Peculiar integrity all their own underlaid

With something with the spark of beautiful
In a special marginal realm that radiated,

On prolonged second glance, quietly—
Serenely.

Of the First Magnitude

Over neighboring and distant
Lands,
Life shimmers in a multitude of colors, often
Connected only by a surface road not a
Path connecting penitent thoughts,
Sorrow, tears, joy or prideful celebrations.

Even though they all see the aurora borealis,
Interpretations may fragment
Into images bred by their own locale—
Beliefs sustaining and bridling but
Which nurture a disconnect that some
May secretly dream of overcoming.

And some do, but gene pools pull tight
Making encounters of the aspirational kind
With the Other a Sisyphean task that only
The boldest of mavericks dare in their
Attempts to reconfigure
What It is.

The only thing remaining
Is to content oneself with
Not knowing everything but
Knowing that things are
Just as they are.

About the Author

Stephen Anderson is an award-winning poet/writer who resides in Milwaukee, Wisconsin. His work has appeared in Southwest Review, Verse Wisconsin, Free Verse, New Purlieu Review, Tipton Poetry Journal, Harvests of New Millennium, Wisconsin Poets' Calendar, Fox Cry Review, Brawler, Foundling Review, The Milwaukee Journal Sentinel as well as in numerous other online and print publications. He has read his work in Milwaukee, Madison and in other cities in Wisconsin, as well as in New York City. He is the author of Montezuma Resurrected And Other Poems (2001) ,The Silent Tango of Dreams, published in June 2006 by Pudding House Publications. His most recent chapbook, Navigating in the Sun, was published by Finishing Line Press (Summer, 2015.) Many of Anderson's poems have been featured on the Milwaukee NPR-affiliate WUWM Lake Effect Program. Several poems of his are included in the poetry collection, Portals And Piers (2012). In the summer of 2013, six of his poems formed the text for a chamber music composition entitled The Privileged Secrets of the Arch performed by two members of the Milwaukee Symphony Orchestra in addition to two other musicians and an opera singer.

The poet also has numerous essays and feature articles to his credit that appeared in the Milwaukee Journal Sentinel and other local and national publications. Anderson is not classifiable as a regional poet per se, although some of his poems relate to Milwaukee and the Midwest. To a large extent, his poetry reflects the poet's travels and residence abroad as a Peace Corps Volunteer in Chile, a university lecturer at Queen Mary & Westfield College (University of London), and numerous trips to Europe and the Caribbean (Trinidad & Tobago), his wife's native country.

www.ingramcontent.com/pod-product-compliance
Lightning Source LLC
Chambersburg PA
CBHW071105090426
42737CB00013B/2486

* 9 7 8 1 9 4 5 7 5 2 6 3 6 *